My Footprints

Majella Ritchie

BookLeaf Publishing
India | USA | UK

Presentation by *BookLeaf Publishing*

Web: www.bookleafpub.com

E-mail: info@bookleafpub.com

ISBN: 9789363317826

First edition 2024

To Mikayla, Lyle, Stephen, Moesha, Malita, Mikey and Maddison, thank you for teaching me true love about culture and the heart you once gave to a stranger.

To Yannis, Danny, Rowan and Heidi, thank you for teaching me the forever impact a student can have on their teacher. May you fly high my angels.

To Aunty Maud and Uncle Jack, thank you for guiding me in a world that was new to me. Your passion for our mob will forever inspire me.

To my best friend Chloe, thank you for being the sister I needed and for always believing in me.

To my Mum, thank you for showing me what strength and resilience looks like. Thank you for inspiring me to continue to show love for every child I meet.

Acknowledgements

I would like to acknowledge the Aboriginal and Torres Strait Islander Peoples of Australia and pay my respects to my Elders, past, present and emerging. I would like to honour the First Nations Children that I continue to have the pleasure of teaching and learning from. May we pave a pathway that is committed towards healing, reconciliation, and a better tomorrow for our Jarjums.

I wake up to the sun rise

No matter where I am, I always see the same skies

I have no place to call home

My footprints continue to roam

I remember them coming to take me away

I still hear my mum's haunting cries

Take me back to her, I would beg and pray

Two years old and they cut all my family ties

Who am I, you ask?

My identity is nothing but a government issued mask

I was given to stranger after stranger

Too many that I've lost count

They all gave me back because they consider me
a 'Child of Danger'

"You're too hard," is all they would shout

Passed on faster before they could learn my
name

Blown from their minds like the smoke to a
flame

The Jarjums around me aren't the same

I look and feel different causing me shame

They point and stare

Like my skin colour is forbidden and rare

Another school, a different day

The same treatment on replay

I don't fit their perfect white box

They don't know what it's like to be surrounded
by grog and gunshots

I am told to act like them

Forget the roots of who I am

My footprints starting to fade

My identity blown away like a grenade

Holes and discolouring in my shirt

A plastic bag and shoes full of dirt

They tell me to look them in the eye

I remind them that respect is something you cannot buy

The letters and numbers run from my brain

I grasp to the culture running through my vein

They don't know how to help me

They look at me and all they see

Is a bad child who never smiles

But don't worry, I'll only be your problem for a short while

The bell rings and I hear everyone cheer

I can only feel my stomach stuck in fear

They all run to their loving hugs and cars

Whilst I hold onto my pain and scars

The workers go in and out

I can't cry anymore, my tears fallen into a drought

I live in a world where I do not belong

This emptiness I feel is so wrong

It's easier to run a muck

Than stay in a busy place where I feel stuck

The rush I feel on the run

Makes me feel like I cannot come undone

The streets is where I find a place to belong

It's the only time I meet others who sing the same song

The cold and dark nights strangely make me feel warm

My footprints lingering in this life storm

I stop and wonder what a home feels like

Maybe a bed, parents and even a bike

I wonder if my mum thinks of me

Surrounded by concrete, she will never be free

My heart beats fast

I run pretending to escape from the past

Dodging the flashing blue and red lights

Met with a figure reading me my rights

I hear yelling, sirens and feel the cuffs of steel

I am met yet again with a justice deal

Funny how it's the only time adults surround to help

Little do they know it's me just trying to yelp

Am I destined for the same future as my mum?

I don't even know what I've become

I remember the stories of my pop

The truth telling of my mob he would often drop

Yarning and 'Shake a leg' he would show

Dear Pop, I promise to never let these memories go

I am again shipped off to another place with no
connection,

No ancestors or bloodstream

Leaving me an empty aggression

Only to be left with what I dream

Walking again into a cold house with no familiar
face

I squint and plead for sanity and grace

Which adult was told I am their new case

They will soon learn, I can escape this place

But this time, something surprises me

I smell the well-known Bushells Tea

I look up and she smiles and says "Come to me"

Her grey hair tells me she's wise

Her words make my heart and spirit rise

My soul suddenly feels a strong light

I walk towards her knowing this feels right

She puts out her hand and pulls me near

She says "I know you've had a rough year,

It's time you feel safe again bub"

Tears begin to well as I grab my eyes to rub

She tells me, "I am here to stay,

You will no longer feel like a lost stray"

She teaches me about language, history and dance

For the first time, my identity is given a chance

The sirens and cuffs of steel all begin to fade

Slowly a new message starts to convey

I am connected to the Kangaroo and Owl

Brought to this earth by a Rainbow Serpent

I come from a line of hunters on the prowl

Strong ancestors that were once raised as a servant

But she tells me I can break the cycle

Start by changing your title

You see she started to piece back my heart

Starting my new footprints on the right path

I know who I am because of her

So if you ask me dear Sir

When I look up to the skies

I will tell you culture is my prize

My old footprints left behind

With new ones leading the path for the culturally
blind

I still wake up to the same skies

But this time with ancestral pride

Thanks to the one who made me heal

And gave me a new life deal

So wherever I now go

I will always know

My name is Rowan Daniel a proud Blak Man

All thanks to a woman I now call Nan

Remember our footprints are what matter

Documenting the rises and each fracture

Being taken away is my history

But my culture will always solve my identity
mystery

To the Jarjums reading this

Whatever in life you have missed

It's never too late to change your ways

Rely on your culture and your ancestors in your
days

You can do this, I believe in you.

I know this to be oh so true.